ANIMALS OF THE FOREST

Text by E. Mora

Illustrations by Kennedy

Translated by Jean Grasso Fitzpatrick

BARRON'S

New York/London/Toronto/Sydney

THE WOODPECKER

The woodpecker is an energetic bird. It is a tireless worker and can hammer all day long.

This bird has a strong, cone-shaped beak, lovely stripes, and a pair of broad wings. And it also has a very long tongue! But this tongue doesn't make the woodpecker a chatterbox. It's a rather sticky tongue. After the bird has pecked holes in tree bark with its beak, it sticks its tongue into the holes. That's how it catches insects to eat for dinner.

The woodpecker is a noisy bird. It has a loud call, and when it flies it is anything but quiet. Besides, it is always drumming its beak on tree trunks!

Every day, the woodpecker carefully inspects a tree from top to bottom. When it finds a spot where the worms or insects have eaten into the wood, it starts tapping with its beak. In the spring, the woodpecker also uses its beak to make a nest in the hollow of the tree. But whatever the season, the woodpecker is always in motion—it works hard all day long, and rests only at night.

The woodpecker is an excellent climber. But when it can't find enough insects to eat in the trees, it walks on the ground searching for ants.

The woodpecker is a playful bird. After the eggs hatch, the whole woodpecker family happily plays hide-and-seek high among the tree branches.

THE MOLE

The mole is an expert digger and miner. First it drills its pointed snout, which looks almost like a little elephant trunk, into the ground. Then it quickly digs long tunnels with its wide paws, which look like little spades.

The mole has dark, shining eyes that are as small as pinheads. Since it is almost blind, it can barely tell day from night. Its body is very round, and it has a short tail.

The mole lives and works underground. It is always busy digging tunnels, even when the ground is cold and hard. That is how it finds the insects and worms it eats. It stops just long enough to eat, then goes right back to work.

This animal is always very hungry. It could not survive long without eating—not even for one day. So you see it really must always dig in search of food. Sometimes, at night or even during the day, the mole runs quickly out of its tunnel for a breath of fresh air, or to catch snails and frogs for dinner. But going out for a walk doesn't always turn out to be a good idea. The poor mole! It has a hard time escaping from the foxes and owls.

THE OWL

The owl is an expert night hunter. This bird looks bigger than it really is because it has so many soft feathers, which it keeps puffed up.

The owl has a large head and a flat face. It has two tufts of feathers above its big, yellow eyes, and a short beak that is hooked and very strong.

During the day the owl hides. It perches on a tree branch or in the hollow of a tree trunk and stays so still that it seems to be dozing. But if it hears the least little noise, it opens its big eyes wide and looks all around.

When night falls, the owl goes hunting. Whoo! Whoo! it calls, as it swoops through the dark. Because it has such soft feathers the owl can fly very quietly. So it can easily surprise its prey—the reptiles, mice, squirrels, moles, hares, and rabbits that it needs to eat.

But the owl is a bird of prey with a kind heart. If it finds an abandoned baby owl it will raise it as its own.

When this bird is attacked, it pricks up the feathers on its head and spreads its wings. That makes it look so dangerous that the enemy usually gets scared and goes away.

THE FAWN

It's May, and a fawn has just been born in the forest. How sweet this baby deer looks! It has big ears, a golden red coat with soft white spots on its back, and a short tail.

The mother deer is called a doe. She is so tender with her little one: She cleans it gently with her tongue and feeds it her milk. She shelters it among the leaves of a bush. And she watches it try weakly to stand up on its long, thin legs.

But it doesn't take long for the fawn to grow strong. In a few weeks it is trotting through the forest after its mother. The doe is always searching around for tender grass and buds to eat, so every day the little deer has a new home in a different bush.

The fawn, like all children, loves to play. If a little boy fawn meets a little girl fawn, he chases her. If she tries to hide in the forest, he keeps looking until he finds her.

One day he will be a stag with splendid antlers and a strong and agile body. How majestic he will look!

THE PORCUPINE

Even though the porcupine is covered with hard, sharp quills, it is not at all mean or nasty. It is peace-loving and gentle, and it never attacks other animals.

When it is frightened—and that happens often—the porcupine protects itself by rolling up into a ball. Very few animals dare to touch that prickly ball! The porcupine doesn't worry about snakes, either, because their poison can't hurt it.

If another animal *does* attack the porcupine, however, it pricks up its quills, grunts like a piglet, and starts to shake all over. Then quills fly off its body like sharp swords. They stab the enemy and make it run away.

THE FOX

The fox is shrewd and clever, but also cautious and patient. It is an excellent hunter and a real rascal. It has a pointed snout, big ears that stand straight up, a long, bushy tail, and thick fur.

The fox doesn't dig its own hole. Instead, it prefers to take over the badger's hole—after it chases the badger away, of course. During the day the fox hides out in this hole and snoozes. But at night the fox goes hunting! It uses its sharp eyes, nose, and ears to catch mice, hedgehogs, squirrels, and moles.

The fox is especially fond of birds. It destroys their nests so that it can eat their eggs, and it catches them by leaping on them when they are flying low.

In areas where people live, the fox shows how clever it is by making night raids on henhouses and rabbit-hutches. Then it steals away the hens and rabbits.

The fox's favorite foods usually have either two wings or four paws. But what does it do when it is hungry and doesn't have a bird or a squirrel within "paw's reach"? It goes fishing! The fox waits on the bank of a river or stream. As soon as it sees a fish dart near the surface, it gives the fish a swift whack with its paw. The fish spurts right out of the water, and the fox knows it won't go hungry.

THE LITTLE BEAR

The little bear is smart, lively, and a real joker. When it is born, in the winter, it looks like a little furry ball, and it does little except drink its mother's milk. But before long the little bear grows. Soon it is covered with a thick, soft, fur coat. In the spring, when it comes out of its cave, it can already follow the mother bear around. She teaches it how to find food, sniff out danger, and defend itself.

The little bear soon learns to eat flowers, tender buds, mushrooms, fruit, fish, and—best of all—honey. As soon as it discovers a beehive it goes to work trying to take it over. The bear doesn't worry about the bees because its coat protects it from their stings. It shakes them off by rubbing against a tree trunk or rolling on the ground. This greedy animal sticks its whole face into the beehive, and then eats the honey right along with the honeycombs and the bees that fly under its nose.

The little bear is a sleepyhead, too. At the beginning of winter it gets lazy and sleeps almost straight through until spring.

THE RACCOON

The raccoon is as happy and willful as a monkey and, like the monkey, prefers to stay up in the trees.

The raccoon has a strong body and a pointed face with two black rings around its eyes. Its coat is thick and its tail has pretty black-and-white stripes.

When it goes hunting for reptiles, worms, insects, and mice, the raccoon walks with its nose to the ground. As soon as it sniffs out its prey, it quickly kills it. But the raccoon is an animal with good manners—before it eats, it washes and scrubs its food in water! It uses its forepaws as though they were hands.

The raccoon is also a good swimmer. It can catch fish by sticking out a paw at just the right moment.

People are not always happy to see the raccoon. If it visits a farm, it kills chickens and rabbits. And before the visit is over, the raccoon makes a stop at the orchard. After all, it's nice to have a piece of fruit after dinner!

THE SQUIRREL

The squirrel is a happy, curious animal. It has bright eyes, a round head, and a pointy nose. Its reddish fur is thick and soft. Its beautiful tail is curved and pointed at the tip, like a feather.

It's fun to watch a squirrel eat walnuts and hazelnuts. First it sits down on its hind legs and brings the food to its mouth with its forepaws. It breaks up the shell, using its teeth as a chisel, and throws it away. Then it gobbles up the tastiest part of the nut.

The squirrel loves to watch everything that is going on in the forest. It climbs up tree trunks in a wink and leaps quickly from one branch to another like an acrobat.

The tree is the squirrel's best friend. High in the branches, it has fun with its squirrel playmates, doing daredevil leaps and dives. The squirrel builds its summer nest in the branches, and in a hollow of the trunk makes a cozy house where it can take its long winter rest. In the fall, it fills this house with walnuts, hazelnuts, acorns, and pine nuts. This supply of food will last all winter long, until spring finally arrives.

THE FROG

The frog lives in freshwater streams and ponds and likes nothing better than warming itself in the bright sunshine. It loves the pond. High grasses grow all around, and water lilies with big leaves float on the surface of the water.

You may hear the frog croaking near small streams and bogs, or anywhere else it finds enough water.

The frog eats insects that it catches with its long, sticky tongue.

On warm days, the frog comes out of the water and looks around. It has big eyes that stick out, and a short, flat head. If everything is peaceful, it jumps onto a lily pad or a rock and dozes off. But if it hears a suspicious noise or sees a tasty-looking insect, it dives into the water and swims fast, kicking with its powerful hind legs.

When evening falls, or after a rain, the frog gets together with its other frog friends in the pond. Together they give a concert: ribit! ribit!

THE LITTLE HARE

The little hare is a good jumper and a fast runner. It is a real escape artist. Running away is its most important skill, because that is how it survives enemy attacks.

The hare has a cottonball tail that is white on top. Its teeth are as sharp as a knife, and they are good for gnawing. The hare looks a little bit like a rabbit, but its ears and hind legs are longer.

A baby hare is born with its eyes open. Its body is covered with soft fur. The mother hare feeds it milk for two weeks.

But her little one grows up very fast. When it is just one year old it is already an adult.

The little hare doesn't dig a hole to live in but is happy to find a quiet place to rest during the day. It searches for food only at night, and eats alfalfa and clover.

This animal sleeps very little because it's always on the lookout. It has very good hearing, so it can pick up even the slightest noise. It escapes from danger with a fast zig-zag run, first in one direction and then the other. This way it sometimes manages to escape attacks by foxes, hounds, and birds of prey.

THE BEAVER

The beaver is the engineer of the forest.

It has small eyes, round ears, and a chunky body. Its brownish red coat is fine and soft, with long, shiny bristles.

Its teeth and paws are the tools the beaver uses to build dams, canals, and houses. It eats roots and bark, and when it needs food or lumber for building, it just cuts down trees. It does this by gnawing and gnawing at the bottom of the tree trunks. That way it can even cut down very big trees.

When the beaver swims, it steers by using its wide, flat tail as a rudder. And in case of danger, it sounds the alarm for its beaver friends by slapping its tail on the water or the ground.

The beaver might seem like a crazy engineer because it builds its house so that one part is always dry and one part is always flooded. But for a beaver this is the ideal home. This animal even builds dams to raise the water level at its "front door." That is where it keeps its supply of food for the winter.

THE SKUNK

The skunk is a nice little animal. It seems shy and defenseless, but it is really not afraid of any animal, not even the most ferocious.

It has a round head with a slightly long snout and bright eyes. Its body is long and slender. It has small paws and a wonderful tufted tail. Its fur is black, with long white stripes. This fur is thick and soft.

The skunk lives in a tree hollow or in a hole it has dug in the ground. It sleeps all day, and at night goes hunting for small birds, mice, and squirrels.

When it is hungry and there is a farm nearby, the skunk raids the henhouses and rabbit-hutches. If guard dogs hear it and try to attack, the skunk can defend itself. It raises its beautiful tail and sprays the dogs with a liquid that burns their eyes and makes them run away because of its awful smell. This works very well against other enemies, too!

THE ROBIN

The robin is a little bird that people call "Robin Redbreast." This is because of the bright, red color of its neck and throat.

This bird is very curious. It flies from branch to branch, stopping every so often to watch everything that's going on in the forest.

It eats insects and makes its nest in the most hidden places— the hollows of trees and the densest bushes.

The robin is one of the best singers of all the birds. It sings all year long. It even knows how to whistle! The robin's song is sometimes sweet and sometimes loud. On nice winter days, it warbles very happily. What a cheery sound!